contents

British & North American Readers:
Please note that Australian cup and
spoon measurements are metric. A quick
conversion guide appears on page 63.
A glossary explaining unfamiliar terms
and ingredients begins on page 60.

2 low-fat nibblies

When dinner seems like an interminably long time away, and your belly is growling furiously, these delicious munchies will seem heaven-sent.

vegetable sticks with yogurt dip

1 medium carrot (120g)

2 trimmed celery sticks (150g)

1 medium red capsicum (200g)

1 lebanese cucumber (130g), seeded

200g low-fat yogurt

1 small clove garlic, crushed

1 tablespoon finely chopped fresh mint

1 tablespoon finely chopped fresh chives

Cut carrot, celery, capsicum and cucumber into 8cm-long sticks. Serve vegetable sticks with combined remaining ingredients.

SERVES 4
Per serving
1.1g fat; 253kJ

tomato, basil and bocconcini bites

12 cherry tomatoes, halved

1 tablespoon balsamic vinegar

12 baby bocconcini (120g), halved

24 baby basil leaves

freshly ground black pepper

Combine tomatoes and vinegar in small bowl, cover; stand 10 minutes. Drain tomatoes over small bowl; discard vinegar.
Thread tomato, bocconcini and basil leaves onto toothpicks; top with pepper.

MAKES 24
Per serving 0.8g fat; 48kJ

crispy wedges

4 x 20cm wheat tortillas

2 teaspoons tandoori paste

2 teaspoons basil pesto

Preheat oven to moderate.
Spread one side of two tortillas with tandoori paste; spread pesto over one side of remaining tortillas. Cut each tortilla into 10 wedges, place on oven trays.
Bake, uncovered, in moderate oven about 10 minutes or until crisp. Cool on trays.

MAKES 40
Per serving 0.4g fat; 65kJ

starters

char-grilled
vegetable stack
with tomato dressing

5

1 medium red
capsicum (200g)

1 medium yellow
capsicum (200g)

1 medium
eggplant (300g)

1 tablespoon salt

1 medium
kumara (400g)

1/4 cup (20g) flaked
parmesan cheese

2 teaspoons fresh
thyme leaves

1/2 teaspoon cracked
black pepper

tomato dressing

1/2 cup (125ml)
tomato juice

2 teaspoons
balsamic vinegar

1 clove garlic,
crushed

few drops
Tabasco sauce

Quarter capsicums; remove and discard seeds and membranes. Roast under grill or in very hot oven, skin-side up, until skin blisters and blackens. Cover capsicum with plastic or paper for 5 minutes; peel away and discard skin.

Cut eggplant into eight slices lengthways, place in colander. Sprinkle with salt; stand 30 minutes. Rinse eggplant under cold water; drain on absorbent paper.

Cut kumara in half lengthways, then cut each half into four pieces lengthways; boil, steam or microwave until just tender.

Cook eggplant and kumara, in batches, on heated oiled grill plate (or grill or barbecue) until browned both sides and tender.

Arrange kumara on serving plates, top with eggplant, capsicum and cheese. Drizzle over tomato dressing; sprinkle with thyme and pepper.

Tomato Dressing Combine ingredients in screw-topped jar; shake well.

SERVES 4
Per serving 2.1g fat; 541kJ

6 broad bean and corn soup

1.5kg broad beans, shelled

6 trimmed fresh corn cobs (1.5kg)

1 large carrot (180g)

1 tablespoon peanut oil

1½ tablespoons grated fresh ginger

3 cloves garlic, crushed

2 litres (8 cups) chicken stock

1½ tablespoons light soy sauce

2 green onions, sliced thinly

½ cup (40g) bean sprouts

Boil, steam or microwave beans until just tender. Drain; refresh under cold water then remove and discard outer skins.
Cut corn from cobs; cut carrot into matchstick-sized pieces.
Heat oil in large saucepan; cook ginger and garlic, stirring, 1 minute. Add stock and sauce, bring to a boil. Add beans, corn and carrot; simmer, uncovered, about 5 minutes or until corn is tender.
Just before serving, stir onion and sprouts into soup.

SERVES 6
Per serving 6.5g fat; 1499kJ

steamed garlic and herb mussels

80 medium black
mussels (2kg)

2 tablespoons olive oil

8 cloves garlic,
crushed

4 red thai chillies,
seeded, chopped finely

1 tablespoon finely
grated lemon rind

1 cup (250ml)
lemon juice

1 cup (250ml)
dry white wine

1/2 cup finely chopped
fresh flat-leaf parsley

1/3 cup finely chopped
fresh basil leaves

Scrub mussels; remove beards.
Heat oil in large saucepan; cook garlic, chilli and rind, stirring,
about 2 minutes or until fragrant. Add mussels, juice and wine;
bring to a boil. Cook, covered, about 5 minutes or until mussels
open (discard any that do not). Remove mussels from pan.
Bring pan liquid to a boil; cook, uncovered, about 10 minutes
or until mixture thickens slightly. Stir in parsley and basil.
Return mussels to pan; simmer, stirring, until heated through.

SERVES 8
Per serving 5.9g fat; 514kJ

8 zucchini flowers

filled with suppli rice

2 teaspoons olive oil

*1 small brown onion
(80g), chopped finely*

1 clove garlic, crushed

*1/2 cup (100g)
arborio rice*

*1/4 cup (60ml)
dry white wine*

*1 1/2 cups (375ml)
chicken stock*

*1/4 cup (20g) finely
grated parmesan
cheese*

*50g low-fat fetta
cheese, chopped
coarsely*

*18 fresh zucchini
flowers (250g)*

*150g baby
spinach leaves*

*1/3 cup loosely packed
fresh basil*

*1/3 cup loosely packed
fresh flat-leaf parsley*

*2 teaspoons
balsamic vinegar*

*1 tablespoon
olive oil, extra*

*2/3 cup (50g) flaked
parmesan cheese*

Preheat oven to very hot.

Heat oil in medium saucepan; cook onion and garlic, stirring, until onion is soft. Add rice, wine and stock, bring to a boil; simmer, uncovered, stirring occasionally, about 12 minutes or until rice is tender and liquid is absorbed. Stir in grated parmesan and fetta; cool.

Remove and discard stamens from centre of zucchini flowers; fill flowers with rice mixture, twist petal tops to enclose filling. Place filled flowers on oiled oven trays.

Bake, uncovered, in very hot oven about 15 minutes or until browned lightly and heated through.

Meanwhile, combine spinach, basil and parsley in medium bowl; toss with combined vinegar and extra oil. Serve zucchini flowers with spinach salad; sprinkle with flaked parmesan.

SERVES 6
Per serving 10.1g fat; 830kJ

10 gazpacho

1 litre (4 cups) tomato juice

10 medium egg tomatoes (750g), chopped coarsely

2 medium red onions (340g), chopped coarsely

2 cloves garlic, quartered

1 lebanese cucumber (130g), chopped coarsely

2 tablespoons sherry vinegar

1 medium red capsicum (200g), chopped coarsely

1 small red onion (100g), chopped finely, extra

1 lebanese cucumber (130g), chopped finely, extra

1 small red capsicum (150g), chopped finely, extra

1 tablespoon finely chopped fresh dill

Blend or process juice, tomato, onion, garlic, cucumber, vinegar and capsicum, in batches, until pureed. Cover; refrigerate 3 hours or overnight.

Just before serving, divide soup among serving bowls; stir equal amounts of extra onion, extra cucumber, extra capsicum and dill into each bowl.

SERVES 6
Per serving 0.4g fat; 366kJ

1/4 teaspoon wasabi

2 teaspoons
kecap manis

2 teaspoons
rice vinegar

1 tablespoon
lime juice

1 tablespoon finely
chopped, drained
pickled ginger slices

1/4 teaspoon
sesame oil

1 tablespoon
peanut oil

1 tablespoon water

1/2 sheet toasted nori

24 medium oysters on
the half shell (1.5kg)

1 tablespoon drained
pickled ginger slices,
sliced finely, extra

Whisk wasabi, kecap manis, vinegar, juice, ginger, oils and the
water in small bowl for dressing.
Cut nori in half lengthways; shred finely.
Arrange oysters on serving plate; drizzle with dressing, sprinkle
with nori and extra ginger.

SERVES 4
Per serving 6.2g fat; 326kJ

12 spicy squid salad

10 small uncleaned
squid (1.2kg)

2 tablespoons
finely chopped
fresh lemon grass

1/2 cup (125ml) sweet
chilli sauce

1 clove garlic, crushed

1 tablespoon
peanut oil

1/4 cup (60ml)
lemon juice

100g mizuna

1 cup (80g) bean
sprouts

1/3 cup firmly packed
fresh mint leaves

3 medium tomatoes
(570g), seeded,
chopped finely

Gently pull the head and entrails away from the body of the squid. Remove the clear backbone (quill) from inside the body. Remove side flaps and skin from squid with salted fingers; discard. Wash hoods thoroughly.
Cut hoods down centre to open out. Cut each hood into three triangles, score inside of each squid triangle in a diagonal pattern.
Combine squid with lemon grass, sauce, garlic, oil and juice in large bowl. Cover; refrigerate 3 hours or overnight. Drain squid over small saucepan; reserve marinade.
Cook squid, in batches, on heated oiled grill plate (or grill or barbecue) until curled and tender.
Meanwhile, bring the marinade to a boil; boil, uncovered, 1 minute.
Arrange mizuna, sprouts and mint on serving plates. Top with tomato and squid, drizzle with hot marinade.

SERVES 6
Per serving 6.2g fat; 928kJ

14 grilled asparagus,
prosciutto and peach salad

3 large peaches (660g)

6 slices prosciutto (90g)

500g asparagus,
trimmed

2 tablespoons
lemon juice

2 teaspoons olive oil

100g mizuna

Preheat oven to hot. Cut peaches into quarters, discarding seed.
Cut each slice of prosciutto in half lengthways. Wrap peach quarters
in prosciutto, place on oven tray. Bake, uncovered, in hot oven about
10 minutes or until prosciutto is crisp.
Meanwhile, cook asparagus on heated oiled grill plate (or grill or barbecue)
until browned and just tender; drizzle with combined lemon juice and oil.
Place mizuna on serving plates; top with lemon-coated asparagus
and prosciutto-wrapped peaches.

SERVES 4
Per serving 4.4g fat; 480kJ

steamed chicken
gow gees

2 dried shiitake
mushrooms

500g minced chicken

2 green onions,
chopped finely

1 tablespoon finely
chopped fresh
garlic chives

2 cloves garlic,
crushed

2 teaspoons grated
fresh ginger

$1/4$ teaspoon
five-spice powder

$3/4$ cup (75g) packaged
breadcrumbs

2 tablespoons
hoisin sauce

1 teaspoon sesame oil

1 egg, beaten lightly

30 gow gee wrappers

1 tablespoon chinese
barbecue sauce

1 tablespoon light
soy sauce

2 tablespoons water

2 teaspoons sweet
chilli sauce

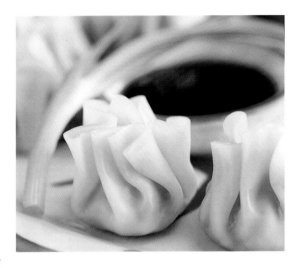

Cover mushrooms with boiling water in heatproof
bowl, stand 20 minutes; drain. Chop caps finely.
Combine mushrooms, chicken, onion, chives,
garlic, ginger, five-spice, breadcrumbs, hoisin
sauce, oil and egg in large bowl. Roll level
tablespoons of chicken mixture into balls;
place on trays. Cover; refrigerate 30 minutes.
Brush wrappers with water, top with chicken
balls; pleat wrappers around balls. Place gow
gees in single layer, 2cm apart, in baking-paper-
lined bamboo steamer. Cook, covered, over wok
of simmering water about 8 minutes or until gow
gees are cooked through. Combine remaining
ingredients in small bowl as a dipping sauce.

MAKES 30
Per serving 2g fat; 243kJ

16 rolled sushi

2 cups (400g)
koshihikari rice

3 cups (750ml)
boiling water

2 tablespoons
rice vinegar

1 tablespoon sugar

1 teaspoon salt

2 teaspoons peanut oil

2 eggs, beaten lightly

1/4 cup (35g) black
sesame seeds

2 sheets toasted nori

1 tablespoon wasabi

1 small red capsicum
(150g), sliced thinly

1 lebanese cucumber
(130g), seeded,
sliced thinly

1 small carrot (70g),
sliced thinly

1 tablespoon
japanese pepper

Place rice in large saucepan with the water; simmer, covered, about 15 minutes or until rice is tender, stirring occasionally. Stir in vinegar, sugar and salt; spread rice on large tray. Refrigerate until cold.

Heat half of the oil in wok or large non-stick frying pan. Add half of the egg, swirl wok so egg forms a thin omelette over base; cook until set, remove, cool. Repeat with remaining oil and egg. Roll omelettes firmly; slice thinly.

Sprinkle a quarter of the sesame seeds on a plastic-wrap-lined bamboo sushi mat. Using wet fingers, pat a quarter of the rice mixture over seeds. Halve nori sheets; place one piece nori on rice. On the narrow side closest to you, spread a quarter of the wasabi in a thin line along edge of nori; cover wasabi with a quarter each of the capsicum, cucumber, carrot and egg strips.

Using narrow side of mat closest to you, start rolling sushi, pressing firmly as you roll. Cut roll into six pieces; sprinkle with pepper. Repeat process with remaining ingredients to make three more rolls; you will have a total of 24 pieces of rolled sushi.

SERVES 8
Per serving 5.4g fat; 1058kJ

mains

white wine risotto 19
with lobster and scallops

1 litre (4 cups)
chicken stock

1 cup (250ml) dry
white wine

1 teaspoon olive oil

1 medium leek
(350g), sliced thinly

2 cloves garlic, crushed

2 cups (400g)
arborio rice

1/2 teaspoon cracked
black pepper

2 tablespoons finely
chopped fresh basil

2 small uncooked
lobster tails (340g)

200g scallops

16 fresh chives

dressing

2 teaspoons
seeded mustard

2 teaspoons olive oil

1 tablespoon
lemon juice

1 tablespoon
chicken stock

1/4 teaspoon sugar

1 tablespoon finely
chopped fresh chives

Combine stock and wine in medium
saucepan. Bring to a boil; cover.
Reduce heat; simmer to keep hot.
Heat oil in large saucepan; cook leek
and garlic, stirring, until leek is soft.
Add rice, stir to coat in oil mixture. Stir
in 1 cup of the hot stock mixture; cook,
stirring, over low heat until liquid is
absorbed. Continue adding stock
mixture, in 1-cup batches, stirring, until
liquid is absorbed after each addition.
Total cooking time should be about
35 minutes or until rice is just tender.
Stir in pepper and basil.
Meanwhile, remove and discard soft
shell from underneath lobster tails to
expose flesh. Cut each lobster tail
in half lengthways. Cook lobster and
scallops on heated oiled grill plate
(or grill or barbecue) until browned all
over and changed in colour.
Serve lobster and scallops on risotto;
drizzle with dressing, top with chives.
Dressing Combine ingredients in
screw-topped jar; shake well.

SERVES 4
Per serving 6.2g fat; 2367kJ

20 pasta and herb salad
with lamb fillets

375g farfalle

250g yellow tear drop tomatoes, halved

1 medium red onion (170g), sliced thinly

50g rocket leaves

1/4 cup finely shredded fresh basil

1 tablespoon fresh thyme leaves

400g lamb fillets

2 cloves garlic, crushed

1 tablespoon seeded mustard

1/4 cup (60ml) balsamic vinegar

Cook pasta in large saucepan of boiling water, uncovered, until just tender; drain.
Combine tomato, onion, rocket, basil and thyme in large bowl.
Rub lamb all over with combined garlic and mustard; cook on heated oiled grill plate (or grill or barbecue) until browned both sides and cooked as desired. Stand 5 minutes; slice thinly.
Add pasta, lamb and vinegar to vegetables; toss to combine.

SERVES 4
Per serving 4.9g fat; 1910kJ

crumbed fish with
warm tomato salad

cooking-oil spray

1 medium red
onion (170g)

250g cherry tomatoes

1/4 cup (60ml) white
wine vinegar

2 cloves garlic,
crushed

1/3 cup (55g) corn
flake crumbs

1 teaspoon
ground cumin

1 teaspoon
sweet paprika

1 teaspoon ground
turmeric

4 firm white fish
fillets (800g)

1/4 cup (35g) plain flour

2 egg whites,
beaten lightly

150g baby
spinach leaves

1/4 cup (50g)
drained capers

Preheat oven to hot. Lightly spray oven tray with cooking oil. Cut onion into thin wedges. Place onion and tomato on tray; drizzle with combined vinegar and garlic. Bake, uncovered, in hot oven about 20 minutes or until tomatoes are soft.
Combine crumbs and spices in small bowl.
Meanwhile, coat fish in flour; shake away excess. Dip fish in egg white, coat in crumb mixture. Spray fish both sides with cooking oil; cook, uncovered, in heated large non-stick frying pan until browned both sides and cooked through.
Combine spinach and capers in large bowl with tomato and onion mixture; serve with fish.

SERVES 4
Per serving 5.8g fat; 1421kJ

22 mustard veal with
polenta and spinach puree

1/3 cup (95g)
seeded mustard

2 tablespoons
coarsely chopped
fresh oregano

2 cloves garlic,
crushed

4 veal chops (600g)

4 large egg tomatoes
(360g), halved
lengthways

2 cups (500ml) water

1 teaspoon salt

1 cup (170g) polenta

3/4 cup (180ml)
skim milk

1/4 cup (20g) finely
grated parmesan
cheese

2kg spinach, trimmed

2 cloves garlic,
crushed, extra

2 anchovy fillets,
drained

2 tablespoons
lemon juice

1/4 cup (60ml)
beef stock

Combine mustard, oregano and garlic in small bowl; brush veal both sides with mustard mixture.
Cook veal and tomato, in batches, on heated oiled grill plate (or grill or barbecue) until veal is browned both sides and cooked as desired and tomato is browned and tender.
Meanwhile, bring the water and salt to a boil in medium saucepan. Stir in polenta; cook, stirring, about 10 minutes or until polenta thickens. Stir in milk; cook, stirring, about 5 minutes or until polenta thickens. Stir in cheese.
Boil, steam or microwave spinach until just wilted; squeeze out excess liquid with hands. Blend or process spinach with remaining ingredients until pureed.
Serve veal chops with tomato, polenta and pureed spinach.

SERVES 4
Per serving 7.3g fat; 1626kJ

24 salmon with dill
and caper dressing

2 tablespoons low-fat sour cream

1 tablespoon drained tiny capers

2 teaspoons coarsely chopped fresh dill

2 teaspoons horseradish cream

1 teaspoon lime juice

4 small salmon fillets (600g)

Combine sour cream with capers, dill, horseradish and juice in medium bowl.
Cook salmon on heated oiled grill plate (or grill or barbecue) until browned both sides and cooked as desired.
Serve salmon with dill and caper dressing.

SERVES 4
Per serving 11.6g fat; 871kJ

char-grilled tuna with

lime and wasabi dressing

4 tuna steaks (800g)

*2 medium limes
(160g), sliced thickly*

cucumber salad

*2 lebanese
cucumbers (260g),
seeded, sliced thinly*

*2 radishes (30g),
trimmed, sliced thinly*

*2 tablespoons
drained pickled
ginger slices*

*1 tablespoon
rice vinegar*

1 teaspoon sugar

wasabi dressing

1/2 teaspoon wasabi

*2 tablespoons
japanese soy sauce*

*2 tablespoons
rice vinegar*

*1 tablespoon
lime juice*

1/2 teaspoon sugar

Cook tuna and lime on heated oiled grill plate (or grill or barbecue) until tuna and lime are browned both sides and tuna is cooked as desired.

Serve tuna with lime on cucumber salad; drizzle with wasabi dressing.

Cucumber Salad Combine ingredients in small bowl, cover; refrigerate 30 minutes. Strain cucumber salad; discard liquid.

Wasabi Dressing Combine ingredients in screw-topped jar; shake well.

SERVES 4
Per serving 12.6g fat; 1448kJ

26 lamb racks with
char-grilled polenta and spicy chutney

4 trimmed lamb racks (780g),
3 cutlets per rack

2 cloves garlic, crushed

1/4 cup (60ml) lemon juice

1 tablespoon honey

1 tablespoon seeded mustard

2 teaspoons finely chopped
fresh thyme

char-grilled polenta

1 1/2 cups (375ml) chicken stock

3/4 cup (180ml) skim milk

1 cup (170g) polenta

1/2 cup (40g) finely grated
parmesan cheese

2 teaspoons finely chopped
fresh thyme

spicy chutney

1 medium red onion (170g),
chopped finely

1 teaspoon curry powder

2 teaspoons seeded mustard

1/2 teaspoon sambal oelek

2 tablespoons dried currants

2 large tomatoes (500g),
chopped coarsely

1/2 cup (100g) brown sugar

1 1/2 tablespoons
balsamic vinegar

Combine lamb in large bowl with
remaining ingredients, cover;
refrigerate 3 hours or overnight.
Preheat oven to hot. Place lamb
in large oiled baking dish; bake,
uncovered, in hot oven about
15 minutes or until cooked as
desired. Cover racks; stand
5 minutes before serving.
Serve lamb with char-grilled
polenta and spicy chutney.
Char-grilled Polenta Heat stock and
milk in large saucepan (do not boil).
Add polenta; cook, stirring, about
2 minutes or until liquid is absorbed
and mixture thickens. Stir in cheese
and thyme. Spoon polenta into deep
19cm-square cake pan, pressing firmly
to ensure even thickness. When cool,
cover; refrigerate about 3 hours or until
firm. Turn polenta onto board, trim
edges; cut into quarters, cut each
quarter into two triangles. Cook polenta
on heated oiled grill plate (or grill or
barbecue) until browned both sides.
Spicy Chutney Combine ingredients in
large saucepan; stir over heat until sugar
dissolves; bring to a boil. Reduce heat;
simmer, uncovered, stirring occasionally,
about 1 hour or until thickened.

SERVES 4
Per serving 14g fat; 1947kJ

28 pork fillet with
apple and leek

800g pork fillets

*³/₄ cup (180ml)
chicken stock*

*2 medium leeks
(700g), sliced thickly*

1 clove garlic, crushed

*2 tablespoons
brown sugar*

*2 tablespoons red
wine vinegar*

*2 medium apples
(300g)*

10g butter

*1 tablespoon brown
sugar, extra*

*400g baby carrots,
trimmed, halved
lengthways*

*8 medium patty-pan
squash (100g),
quartered*

*250g asparagus,
trimmed, chopped
coarsely*

Preheat oven to very hot. Place pork, in single layer, in large baking dish; bake, uncovered, in very hot oven about 25 minutes or until pork is browned and cooked as desired. Cover; stand 5 minutes before slicing thickly.

Meanwhile, heat half of the stock in medium frying pan; cook leek and garlic, stirring, until leek softens and browns slightly. Add sugar and vinegar; cook, stirring, about 5 minutes or until leek caramelises. Add remaining stock; bring to a boil. Reduce heat; simmer, uncovered, about 5 minutes or until liquid reduces by half. Place leek mixture in medium bowl; cover to keep warm.

Peel, core and halve apples; cut into thick slices. Melt butter in same pan; cook apple and extra sugar, stirring, until apple is browned and tender.

Boil, steam or microwave carrot, squash and asparagus, separately, until just tender; drain.

Serve pork, topped with caramelised apple and sweet and sour leek, on top of mixed vegetables.

SERVES 4
Per serving 7.5g fat; 1624kJ

30 cioppino

2 small uncooked blue swimmer crabs (700g)

200g clams

16 large uncooked prawns (500g)

450g swordfish steaks

1 tablespoon olive oil

1 medium brown onion (150g), chopped coarsely

2 trimmed sticks celery (150g), chopped coarsely

3 cloves garlic, crushed

6 medium tomatoes (1kg), chopped coarsely

415g can tomato puree

1/2 cup (125ml) dry white wine

1 1/3 cups (330ml) fish stock

1 teaspoon sugar

200g scallops

2 tablespoons shredded fresh basil

1/3 cup coarsely chopped fresh flat-leaf parsley

To kill crabs humanely, drown them in fresh water or freeze them for 2 hours (any longer will freeze the meat). Then, holding crab firmly, slide a sharp, strong knife under top of shell at back, lever off shell. Remove and discard whitish gills. Rinse well under cold water. Using a cleaver, chop each crab into large pieces.

Scrub clam shells with stiff brush, if necessary, then soak in lightly salted water for a few hours; stir occasionally, or change the water to encourage them to discard their sand.

Shell and devein prawns, leaving tails intact. Chop fish into 2cm pieces.

Heat oil in large saucepan; cook onion, celery and garlic, stirring, until onion is soft. Add tomato; cook, stirring, 5 minutes or until pulpy. Stir in puree, wine, stock and sugar; bring to a boil. Reduce heat; simmer, covered, 20 minutes.

Add crab and clams to pan; simmer, covered, 10 minutes. Discard any clams that do not open. Add prawns, fish and scallops; cook, stirring occasionally, about 5 minutes or until seafood has changed in colour and is cooked through. Stir in herbs.

SERVES 6
Per serving 7.1g fat; 1068kJ

32 braised chicken

breasts with preserved lemon

4 single chicken
breasts on
bone (1kg)

1 medium
leek (350g),
sliced thinly

2 cloves garlic,
crushed

1 tablespoon
finely chopped,
rinsed preserved
lemon

400g baby
carrots,
trimmed, halved
lengthways

1/3 cup (80ml)
dry white wine

1 1/2 cups (375ml)
chicken stock

1 tablespoon
finely chopped
fresh tarragon

200g broccolini,
trimmed

1 tablespoon
thinly sliced,
rinsed preserved
lemon, extra

Remove and discard skin from chicken. Cook chicken, in batches, in heated large oiled saucepan until browned all over. Cook leek, garlic and lemon in same pan, stirring, until fragrant.

Return chicken and juices to pan with carrot, wine, stock and tarragon; bring to a boil. Reduce heat; simmer, covered, 25 minutes or until carrot is tender.

Remove chicken and carrot from pan, cover to keep warm. Return pan to heat; boil, uncovered, 5 minutes or until sauce is reduced to 2 cups.

Boil, steam or microwave broccolini until tender.

Serve chicken on broccolini and carrots; drizzle with sauce, top with extra lemon.

SERVES 4
Per serving 9.1g fat; 1163kJ

with tomatoes and chickpeas

2kg baby octopus

1/3 cup (75g) firmly packed brown sugar

1/4 cup (60ml) tomato sauce

2 tablespoons barbecue sauce

2 tablespoons worcestershire sauce

2 tablespoons malt vinegar

9 medium egg tomatoes (675g), halved lengthways

2 tablespoons balsamic vinegar

2 tablespoons brown sugar, extra

2 tablespoons water

1/2 cup finely chopped fresh mint

2 x 300g cans chickpeas, rinsed, drained

1/4 cup finely chopped fresh coriander

Discard heads and beaks from octopus; cut octopus in half. Combine octopus, half of the sugar, sauces and malt vinegar in large bowl. Cover; refrigerate 3 hours.
Preheat oven to moderate. Combine tomato, balsamic vinegar, remaining sugar, water and half of the mint in large baking dish; bake, uncovered, in moderate oven 45 minutes. Remove tomato from dish, cover to keep warm. Add chickpeas to juices in same dish; simmer, uncovered, 3 minutes or until mixture thickens.
Meanwhile, drain octopus; discard marinade.
Cook octopus, in batches, on heated oiled grill plate (or grill or barbecue) until just tender; combine with remaining mint and coriander. Serve octopus with roasted tomatoes and chickpeas.

SERVES 6
Per serving 2.6g fat; 1096kJ

2 spatchcocks (1kg)

3 cloves garlic, crushed

1 tablespoon grated fresh ginger

2 tablespoons rice vinegar

1 tablespoon fish sauce

1/3 cup (80ml) sweet chilli sauce

1 tablespoon kecap manis

250g baby choy sum, trimmed

1 tablespoon oyster sauce

1/3 cup (80ml) japanese soy sauce

nori rice triangles

1 1/2 cups (300g) koshihikari rice

1/4 cup (60ml) rice vinegar

2 tablespoons sugar

1/4 teaspoon salt

2 sheets toasted nori

Wash spatchcocks under cold water; pat dry with absorbent paper. Using kitchen scissors, cut along both sides of backbones; discard backbones. Cut through breastbones. Carefully remove skin from spatchcock, excluding wings.

Combine halved spatchcocks with garlic, ginger, vinegar, fish sauce, half of the chilli sauce and kecap manis in large bowl. Cover; refrigerate 3 hours or overnight.

Preheat oven to moderate. Drain spatchcock; discard marinade. Place spatchcock on wire rack over baking dish. Bake, uncovered, in moderate oven 25 minutes. Brush spatchcock with remaining chilli sauce; bake, uncovered, a further 10 minutes or until spatchcock is browned and cooked through.

Meanwhile, place choy sum in bamboo steamer, drizzle with oyster sauce; steam, covered, over wok or pan of simmering water until just tender.

Serve spatchcock on choy sum with nori rice triangles and small bowls of soy sauce.

Nori Rice Triangles Line base and sides of a deep 19cm-square cake pan with baking paper. Cook rice in large saucepan of boiling water, uncovered, until just tender. Drain rice; stand 5 minutes. Stir in combined vinegar, sugar and salt. Place one sheet of nori, smooth-side down, in prepared pan; spread rice mixture over nori. Place remaining nori sheet; smooth-side up, over rice, cool in pan. Turn onto board, trim edges; cut into quarters, cut each quarter into two triangles.

SERVES 4
Per serving 12.9g fat; 2386kJ

asian-style barbecued
seafood salad

1kg large uncooked prawns

500g baby octopus

500g small squid hoods

2 cloves garlic, crushed

2 teaspoons grated
fresh ginger

1/4 cup (60ml) lime juice

2 tablespoons oyster sauce

1 tablespoon kecap manis

12cm fresh red thai chilli,
chopped finely

3 cups (240g) shredded
red cabbage

1 cup (80g) bean sprouts

2 tablespoons slivered
almonds, toasted

1 tablespoon white sesame
seeds, toasted

dressing

1 tablespoon sweet
chilli sauce

1/3 cup (80ml) rice vinegar

1/4 cup (60ml) water

2 tablespoons caster sugar

1 teaspoon light soy sauce

Shell and devein prawns, leaving tails intact. Discard heads and beaks from octopus; cut octopus in half. Cut squid hoods in half lengthways; score inside surface of each piece, cut into 5cm-wide strips.

Combine prawns, octopus and squid in large bowl with garlic, ginger, juice, sauces and chilli, cover; refrigerate 3 hours or overnight.

Drain seafood; discard marinade. Barbecue seafood (or grill or char-grill), in batches, until prawns are just changed in colour, and squid and octopus are tender and browned all over.

Serve seafood on combined remaining ingredients; drizzle with dressing.

Dressing Combine ingredients in small saucepan; stir over heat until sugar dissolves. Simmer, uncovered, about 2 minutes or until reduced to 1/2 cup; cool.

SERVES 4
Per serving 7.9g fat; 1536kJ

38 mustard beef
fillet with pumpkin risotto

600g piece beef fillet

1/4 cup (70g) seeded mustard

1 teaspoon honey

1/2 cup (125ml) chicken stock

2 tablespoons dry white wine

1 teaspoon finely chopped fresh oregano

300g asparagus, trimmed

pumpkin risotto

500g piece pumpkin, cut into 2cm pieces

cooking-oil spray

3 1/2 cups (875ml) chicken stock

1/2 cup (125ml) dry white wine

2 teaspoons olive oil

1 medium brown onion (150g), chopped finely

1 clove garlic, crushed

1 1/2 cups (300g) arborio rice

2 tablespoons finely chopped fresh flat-leaf parsley

1/2 teaspoon cracked black pepper

2 tablespoons finely grated parmesan cheese

Preheat oven to moderately hot. Heat oiled flameproof baking dish; brown beef all over. Spread beef with 2 tablespoons of the mustard. Bake beef, uncovered, in moderately hot oven about 30 minutes or until cooked as desired. Remove beef from dish, cover, rest 5 minutes; slice thickly.
Heat same dish, stir in remaining mustard, honey, stock, wine and oregano; cook, stirring, until mixture boils.
Boil, steam or microwave asparagus until just tender. Serve beef on pumpkin risotto, topped with asparagus; drizzle with sauce.
Pumpkin Risotto Spray pumpkin lightly with cooking oil, place on oiled oven tray. Bake, uncovered, in moderately hot oven about 30 minutes or until browned and tender. Combine stock and wine in a medium saucepan. Bring to a boil; cover. Reduce heat; simmer to keep hot. Heat oil in large saucepan; cook onion and garlic, stirring, until onion is soft. Add rice; stir to coat in oil mixture. Stir in 1 cup of the hot stock mixture; cook, stirring, over low heat until liquid is absorbed. Keep adding stock mixture, in 1-cup batches, stirring, until liquid is absorbed after each addition. Total cooking time should be about 35 minutes or until rice is just tender. Gently stir in pumpkin, parsley, pepper and cheese.

SERVES 4
Per serving 13.8g fat; 2643kJ

40 moroccan lamb
with couscous

8 lamb fillets (700g)

1 tablespoon
ground cumin

1 tablespoon
ground coriander

1 teaspoon ground
cinnamon

3/4 cup (210g)
low-fat yogurt

1 1/2 cups (300g)
couscous

1 1/2 cups (375ml)
boiling water

1 teaspoon peanut oil

1/3 cup (50g)
dried currants

2 teaspoons finely
grated lemon rind

2 teaspoons
lemon juice

1/4 cup coarsely
chopped fresh
coriander

Combine lamb, ground spices and half of
the yogurt in medium bowl, cover; refrigerate
3 hours or overnight.
Cook lamb on heated oiled grill plate (or grill or
barbecue) until browned both sides and cooked
as desired. Cover; stand 5 minutes, slice thinly.
Meanwhile, combine couscous, the water
and oil in large heatproof bowl, cover; stand
5 minutes or until liquid is absorbed, fluffing
with fork occasionally. Stir in currants, rind, juice
and fresh coriander; toss with fork to combine.
Serve lamb with couscous; drizzle with
remaining yogurt.

SERVES 4
Per serving 9.3g fat; 2193kJ

beef steaks with

capsicum relish

3 medium red
capsicums (600g)

1 teaspoon olive oil

1 large brown onion
(200g), sliced thinly

2 cloves garlic,
sliced thinly

2 tablespoons
brown sugar

2 tablespoons
sherry vinegar

3 red thai chillies,
seeded, chopped
finely

4 x 200g beef
eye fillet steaks

2 corn cobs (800g),
trimmed, chopped
coarsely

150g sugar snap peas

300g tiny new
potatoes, halved

2 tablespoons finely
chopped fresh
flat-leaf parsley

Quarter capsicums; discard membranes and
seeds. Roast under grill or in very hot oven, skin-
side up, until skin blisters and blackens. Cover
capsicum with plastic or paper for 5 minutes; peel
away and discard skin, slice capsicum thinly.
Heat oil in medium frying pan; cook onion and
garlic, stirring, until soft. Add sugar, vinegar,
chilli and capsicum; cook, stirring, 5 minutes.
Meanwhile, cook beef on heated oiled grill plate
(or grill or barbecue) until browned both sides
and cooked as desired. Boil, steam or microwave
vegetables, separately, until just tender; drain.
Top steaks with capsicum relish; serve with
vegetables, sprinkle with parsley.

SERVES 4
Per serving 13g fat; 2327kJ

42 barramundi

fillets with udon noodles

4 barramundi
fillets (800g)

1/4 teaspoon
five-spice powder

700g udon noodles

50g snow pea sprouts

1/4 cup (35g) shelled
pistachios, coarsely
chopped, toasted

1 tablespoon
white sesame
seeds, toasted

dressing

1 1/2 tablespoons
peanut oil

1/4 cup (60ml) light
soy sauce

1 1/2 tablespoons
rice vinegar

1 small clove
garlic, crushed

1/2 teaspoon
sambal oelek

Sprinkle fish with five-spice-powder. Cook fish in heated oiled large non-stick frying pan until browned both sides and just cooked through.

Meanwhile, place noodles in large heatproof bowl, cover with boiling water, stand about 3 minutes or until just tender; drain. Combine noodles in large bowl with 2 tablespoons of the dressing; toss to combine.

Serve fish on noodles, topped with sprouts; drizzle with remaining dressing. Sprinkle with combined nuts and seeds.

Dressing Combine ingredients in screw-topped jar; shake well.

SERVES 4
Per serving 14.8g fat; 2475kJ

desserts

rich chocolate 45

meringue cake

8 egg whites

1 cup (220g) caster sugar

1/4 cup (25g) cocoa powder

60g dark chocolate, chopped finely

1/4 cup (60g) finely chopped glacé figs

1/4 cup (40g) finely chopped seeded prunes

3/4 cup (50g) stale breadcrumbs

1/3 cup (80ml) thickened light cream (18% fat)

1 tablespoon icing sugar mixture

1 tablespoon cocoa powder, extra

Preheat oven to very slow. Grease 22cm springform pan, line base with baking paper. Flour the side of pan; shake away excess.

Beat egg whites in large bowl with electric mixer until soft peaks form. Gradually add caster sugar, beating until sugar is dissolved between additions.

Fold in sifted cocoa, chocolate, fruit and breadcrumbs. Spoon mixture into prepared pan. Bake, uncovered, in very slow oven about 1 1/2 hours or until firm; cool in oven with door ajar.

Chill small bowl and beaters. Add cream to chilled bowl; beat until soft peaks form.

Dust cake with sifted icing sugar and extra cocoa; serve with cream.

SERVES 8
Per serving 5.8g fat; 1082kJ

46 poached pears in
raspberry and vanilla-bean syrup

6 medium corella
pears (1kg)

1 cup (220g) sugar

2 cups (500ml) water

1 vanilla bean

150g fresh raspberries

3 teaspoons finely
shredded fresh mint

Peel pears, leaving stems intact.

Combine sugar and the water in large saucepan; stir over
heat until sugar dissolves. Split vanilla bean in half lengthways;
scrape seeds into syrup. Add pears and one-third of the
raspberries to pan; bring to a boil. Reduce heat; simmer,
covered, about 20 minutes or until pears are just tender,
turning pears occasionally during cooking, cool.

Place pears and syrup in large bowl. Cover; refrigerate overnight,
turning pears occasionally.

One hour before serving, add remaining raspberries; stir gently
to combine, then refrigerate. Sprinkle mint over pears to serve.

SERVES 6
Per serving 0.2g fat; 896kJ

with honey yogurt

4 medium
quinces (1.3kg)

2 tablespoons
demerara sugar

200g low-fat
honey yogurt

1 tablespoon
demerara sugar, extra

Preheat oven to moderate. Peel, halve and core quinces.
Sprinkle cut side of quinces with sugar. Wrap two halves tightly
in two layers of foil; place in baking dish, repeat with remaining
quince halves. Add a little water to dish.
Bake in moderate oven about 2½ hours or until quinces are
tender and a rich pink colour.
Serve quince halves with honey yogurt, sprinkle with extra sugar.

SERVES 4
Per serving 1.1g fat; 968kJ

48

caramelised
oranges
with ice-cream

4 large oranges (1.2kg)
2 tablespoons brown sugar
2 tablespoons Grand Marnier
200g low-fat vanilla ice-cream

Peel oranges, removing as
much white pith as possible;
cut crossways into thick slices.
Place oranges, in single layer,
on oven tray. Sprinkle with sugar;
drizzle with liqueur.
Cook orange on both sides under
hot grill until just caramelised.
Divide ice-cream and orange
among four serving dishes;
drizzle with pan juices.

SERVES 4
Per serving 3.2g fat; 898kJ

chocolate
raspberry
frozen parfait

1/3 cup (75g) caster sugar

1/4 cup (25g) drinking chocolate

2 tablespoons custard powder

3/4 cup (180ml) skim milk

*1/2 cup (125ml) creamy
evaporated milk, chilled*

100g frozen raspberries

Line 8cm x 26cm bar cake pan with
baking paper, extending paper 5cm
over the edge of the long sides of pan.
Combine sugar, drinking chocolate
and custard powder in small saucepan.
Gradually stir in skim milk until smooth.
Stir over heat until mixture boils
and thickens. Cover surface with
plastic wrap; cool.
Beat evaporated milk in small bowl with
electric mixer until soft peaks form, then
fold into custard mixture with the berries.
Pour mixture into prepared pan, cover;
freeze 8 hours or overnight, until firm.
Serve sliced with extra berries, if desired.

SERVES 4
Per serving 3.2g fat; 773kJ

52 plum

clafouti

1½ cups (375ml) low-fat custard

¼ cup (35g) self-raising flour

1 egg yolk

2 egg whites

825g can whole plums, drained, halved, seeded

2 teaspoons icing sugar mixture

Preheat oven to moderate.
Combine custard, flour and egg yolk in medium bowl; stir until smooth.
Beat egg whites in small bowl with electric mixer on highest speed until soft peaks form; fold into custard mixture. Pour into 24cm-round ovenproof pie dish.
Pat plums dry with absorbent paper, arrange plums, cut-side down, over custard. Place pie dish on oven tray.
Bake, uncovered, in moderate oven about 40 minutes or until firm.
Just before serving, dust with sifted icing sugar.

SERVES 4
Per serving 2.6g fat; 1019kJ

hot
passionfruit
soufflés

1 tablespoon caster sugar

2 egg yolks

½ cup (125ml) passionfruit pulp

1 teaspoon finely grated lemon rind

½ cup (80g) icing sugar mixture

4 egg whites

Preheat oven to moderately hot. Grease six
¾-cup (180ml) soufflé dishes. Sprinkle the bases
and sides evenly with caster sugar; shake away
the excess. Place dishes on oven tray.
Whisk egg yolks with the passionfruit, rind
and 2 tablespoons of the icing sugar in
medium bowl until combined.
Beat egg whites in small bowl with electric mixer
until soft peaks form. Add remaining icing sugar;
continue beating until firm peaks form.
Fold a quarter of the egg white mixture into the
passionfruit mixture, then gently fold in remaining
egg white mixture. Spoon into prepared dishes;
bake in moderately hot oven about 10 minutes
or until soufflés are well risen and browned.
Dust tops with extra sifted icing sugar, if desired.

SERVES 6
Per serving 1.9g fat; 428kJ

lunsciously light
chocolate
mousse

1 1/2 *teaspoons gelatine*

2 *tablespoons water*

1/3 *cup (35g) cocoa powder*

3/4 *cup (180ml) thickened light cream (18% fat)*

3 *egg whites*

1/2 *cup (110g) caster sugar*

25g *lite chocolate*

Sprinkle gelatine over the water in a cup.
Stand the cup in small saucepan of simmering
water, stir until gelatine dissolves. Remove
from pan; cool 5 minutes.
Meanwhile, sift cocoa powder into medium
bowl; whisk in cream until lightly whipped.
Whisk in the gelatine mixture.
Beat egg whites in small bowl with electric mixer
until soft peaks form. Gradually add sugar,
beating until sugar is dissolved between
additions. Fold the egg white mixture into
the chocolate mixture, in two batches.
Divide mixture among six 3/4-cup (180ml) serving
dishes. Cover; refrigerate 3 hours or until set.
Pull a vegetable peeler along the chocolate to
form curls; sprinkle curls over the mousse.

SERVES 6
Per serving 10g fat; 804kJ

58 low-fat coffee treats

If you're following a low-fat diet, you'll be delighted to know there's no need to exclude these little indulgences – perfect treats to serve with coffee.

no-guilt rum balls

1½ cups (150g) chocolate cake crumbs

2 cups (70g) rice bubbles, crushed

¼ cup (40g) sultanas, chopped coarsely

2 tablespoons cocoa powder

2 tablespoons dark rum

½ cup (125ml) sweetened condensed skim milk

½ cup (50g) chocolate sprinkles

Combine crumbs, rice bubbles, sultanas, sifted cocoa, rum and milk in large bowl. Roll level tablespoons of mixture into balls; roll balls in the sprinkles.

Place balls on a tray lined with plastic wrap, cover; refrigerate about 1 hour or until firm.

MAKES 24
Per serving 1.2g fat; 292kJ

meringues

1 egg white

½ teaspoon white vinegar

⅓ cup (75g) caster sugar

1 teaspoon icing sugar mixture

Preheat oven to very slow. Grease oven trays; dust with cornflour, shaking off excess.
Beat egg white, vinegar and caster sugar in small bowl with electric mixer about 10 minutes or until sugar dissolves; fold in icing sugar.
Place meringue mixture into piping bag fitted with small plain tube; pipe 1.5cm rounds 3cm apart onto prepared trays. Bake in very slow oven about 30 minutes or until crisp and dry. Cool meringues on trays.

MAKES 70
Per serving 0g fat; 19kJ

chocolate almond bread

2 egg whites

⅓ cup (75g) caster sugar

¾ cup (110g) plain flour

1 tablespoon cocoa powder

¾ cup (120g) blanched almonds, toasted

Preheat oven to moderate. Lightly grease 8cm x 26cm bar cake pan, line base and sides with baking paper.
Beat egg whites in small bowl with electric mixer until soft peaks form, gradually add sugar, beating until dissolved between additions.
Fold in combined sifted flour and cocoa, then almonds. Spread mixture into prepared pan. Bake, uncovered, in moderate oven about 25 minutes or until browned lightly. Cool in pan, wrap in foil; stand overnight.
Preheat oven to slow. Using a serrated or electric knife, cut the bread into 3mm slices. Place slices in single layer on oven trays. Bake in slow oven about 20 minutes or until crisp and dry; cool on wire racks.

MAKES 70
Per serving 1g fat; 85kJ

glossary

barbecue sauce a spicy, tomato-based sauce used to marinade, baste or as an accompaniment.

blue swimmer crabs also known as sand crabs and Atlantic blue crabs.

bocconcini small rounds of fresh "baby" mozzarella; a semi-soft white cheese. Store under refrigeration, in brine, for one or two days maximum.

breadcrumbs

packaged: fine-textured, crunchy, purchased white breadcrumbs.

stale: stale one- or two-day-old bread made into crumbs by grating, blending or processing.

broad beans also known as fava beans; best eaten when peeled twice (discard both the long pod and the pale-green inner shell.

broccolini milder and sweeter than the traditional broccoli, it is completely edible from flower to stem with a delicate flavour with a subtle, peppery edge. Also known as baby broccoli, broccolini has a long, slender stem.

butter use salted or unsalted (sweet) butter; 125g is equal to one stick of butter.

capers the grey-green buds of a warm-climate shrub; sold either dried and salted or pickled in vinegar brine.

capsicum also known as bell pepper or, simply, pepper. Discard membranes and seeds before use.

chickpeas also known as garbanzos, hummus or channa; an irregularly round, sandy-coloured legume.

choy sum also known as flowering bok choy, flowering white, or chinese flowering, cabbage. The stems, leaves and yellow flowers are all edible.

clams we used a small ridge-shelled variety of this bivalve mollusc; also known as vongole.

couscous a fine, grain-like cereal product, originally from North Africa; made from semolina.

custard powder packaged vanilla pudding mixture.

drinking chocolate sweetened cocoa powder.

eggplant also known as aubergine.

fish sauce also called nam pla or nuoc nam; made from pulverised, salted, fermented fish, most often anchovies.

five-spice powder a fragrant blend of ground cinnamon, cloves, star anise, sichuan pepper and fennel seeds.

flour

plain: an all-purpose flour, made from wheat.

self-raising: plain flour sifted with baking powder in the proportion of 1 cup flour to 2 teaspoons baking powder.

ginger, pickled sweet, pink, pickled ginger, often eaten with sushi and sashimi.

grand marnier orange-flavoured liqueur based on cognac-brandy.

green onion also known as scallion, eschalot and, incorrectly, shallots; an onion picked before the bulb has formed. Has a long, green, edible stalk.

hoisin sauce thick, sweet and spicy Chinese paste made from fermented soy beans, onions and garlic.

horseradish cream paste of grated horseradish, vinegar, oil and sugar.

japanese pepper a mixture of ground spices also known as sichimi togarashi.

kecap manis Indonesian thick soy sauce which has sugar and spices added.

kumara Polynesian name of orange-fleshed sweet potato often confused with yam.

lemons, preserved a North African specialty; fruit is preserved in a mixture of salt and lemon juice. Can be rinsed and eaten as is, or added to casseroles and tagines for a rich salty-sour acidic flavour.

lemon grass a tall, clumping, lemon-smelling and -tasting, sharp-edged grass; the white lower part of the stem is chopped and used.

lobster also known as crayfish.

mizuna a Japanese green salad leaf with a delicate mustard flavour.

mushrooms, dried shiitake to reconstitute, soak in warm water for 15 to 20 minutes; discard hard stems and use caps. Shiitakes have a unique meaty flavour.

noodles, udon available fresh and dried, these Japanese broad white wheat noodles are similar to the ones in homemade chicken noodle soup.

nori dried seaweed used in Japanese cooking as a flavouring, garnish or for sushi. Sold in thin sheets.

oyster sauce made from oysters and their brine, cooked with salt, soy sauce and starches.

polenta a cereal of ground corn (maize); like cornmeal but finer and paler. Also the name of the dish it makes.

prawns also known as shrimp.

prosciutto Salt-cured, air-dried (unsmoked), pressed ham; sold ready to eat.

rice

arborio small, round-grain rice well-suited to absorb a large amount of liquid.

koshihikari small, round-grain, white rice. Substitute white short-grain rice; cook by the absorption method.

rocket also known as arugula, rugula and rucola; peppery-tasting green leaf.

sambal oelek (also ulek or olek) a salty chilli paste.

sesame oil made from crushed sesame seeds; used to add flavour, not as a cooking medium.

spatchcock a small chicken (poussin), up to 6 weeks old, weighing 500g at most.

spinach also known as english spinach and incorrectly, silverbeet.

sugar snap peas also known as honey snap peas; snow peas can be substituted.

sultanas dried grapes; also known as golden raisins.

tomato sauce also known as ketchup or catchup.

tortilla, wheat thin, round unleavened bread.

vinegar

rice: made from fermented rice; flavoured with sugar and salt. Also known as seasoned rice vinegar.

sherry: natural vinegar aged in oak according to the traditional Spanish system.

wasabi an Asian horseradish sauce traditionally served with sashimi and sushi; sold in powdered or paste form.

zucchini also known as courgette. The yellow flowers, sometimes with baby vegetables still attached, are available in specialist greengrocers.

index

facts and figures 63

These conversions are approximate only, but the difference between an exact and the approximate conversion of various liquid and dry measures is minimal and will not affect your cooking results.

Measuring equipment

The difference between one country's measuring cups and another's is, at most, within a 2 or 3 teaspoon variance. (For the record, 1 Australian metric measuring cup holds approximately 250ml.) The most accurate way of measuring dry ingredients is to weigh them. For liquids, use a clear glass or plastic jug having metric markings.

Note: NZ, Canada, USA and UK all use 15ml tablespoons. Australian tablespoons measure 20ml.
All cup and spoon measurements are level.

How to measure

When using graduated measuring cups, shake dry ingredients loosely into the appropriate cup. Do not tap the cup on a bench or tightly pack the ingredients unless directed to do so. Level the top of measuring cups and measuring spoons with a knife. When measuring liquids, place a clear glass or plastic jug having metric markings on a flat surface to check accuracy at eye level.

Dry Measures

metric	imperial
15g	1/2oz
30g	1oz
60g	2oz
90g	3oz
125g	4oz (1/4lb)
155g	5oz
185g	6oz
220g	7oz
250g	8oz (1/2lb)
280g	9oz
315g	10oz
345g	11oz
375g	12oz (3/4lb)
410g	13oz
440g	14oz
470g	15oz
500g	16oz (1lb)
750g	24oz (1 1/2lb)
1kg	32oz (2lb)

We use large eggs having an average weight of 60g.

Liquid Measures

metric	imperial
30ml	1 fluid oz
60ml	2 fluid oz
100ml	3 fluid oz
125ml	4 fluid oz
150ml	5 fluid oz (1/4 pint/1 gill)
190ml	6 fluid oz
250ml (1cup)	8 fluid oz
300ml	10 fluid oz (1/2 pint)
500ml	16 fluid oz
600ml	20 fluid oz (1 pint)
1000ml (1litre)	1 3/4 pints

Helpful Measures

metric	imperial
3mm	1/8in
6mm	1/4in
1cm	1/2in
2cm	3/4in
2.5cm	1in
6cm	2 1/2in
8cm	3in
20cm	8in
23cm	9in
25cm	10in
30cm	12in (1ft)

Oven Temperatures

These oven temperatures are only a guide.
Always check the manufacturer's manual.

	°C (Celsius)	°F (Fahrenheit)	Gas Mark
Very slow	120	250	1
Slow	150	300	2
Moderately slow	160	325	3
Moderate	180 –190	350 – 375	4
Moderately hot	200 – 210	400 – 425	5
Hot	220 – 230	450 – 475	6
Very hot	240 – 250	500 – 525	7

at your fingertips

These elegant slipcovers store up to 10 mini books and make the books instantly accessible.

And the metric measuring cups and spoons make following our recipes a piece of cake.

Book Holder
Australia and overseas:
$A8.95 (incl. GST).

Metric Measuring Set
Australia: $6.50 (incl. GST).
New Zealand: $A8.00.
Elsewhere: $A9.95.
Prices include postage
and handling.
This offer is available
in all countries.

Mail or fax Photocopy and complete the coupon below and post to ACP Books Reader Offer, ACP Publishing, GPO Box 4967, Sydney NSW 2001, or fax to (02) 9267 4967.

Phone Have your credit card details ready, then phone 136 116 (Mon-Fri, 8.00am - 6.00pm; Sat 8.00am - 6.00pm).

Australian residents We accept the credit cards listed on the coupon, money orders and cheques.

Overseas residents We accept the credit cards listed on the coupon, drafts in $A drawn on an Australian bank, and also British, New Zealand and U.S. cheques in the currency of the country of issue.

Photocopy and complete the coupon below

- ☐ **Book holder** ☐ **Metric measuring set**

Please indicate number(s) required.

Mr/Mrs/Ms _____

Address _____

_____

Postcode _____ Country _____

Phone: Business hours ( ) _____

I enclose my cheque/money order for $_____ payable to ACP Publishing

OR: please charge $ _____ to my: ☐ Bankcard ☐ Visa

☐ Amex ☐ MasterCard ☐ Diners Club Expiry Date ___/___

Cardholder's signature _____

Please allow up to 30 days for delivery within Australia.

Allow up to 6 weeks for overseas deliveries. Both offers expire 31/12/02.
HLMLFG02

Food director Pamela Clark
Associate food editor Karen Hammial
Assistant food editor Kathy McGarry
Assistant recipe editor Elizabeth Hooper

ACP BOOKS STAFF
Editorial director Susan Tomnay
Editor Julie Collard
Concept design Jackie Richards
Designer Caryl Wiggins
Publishing manager (sales) Jennifer McDonald
Publishing manager
(rights & new titles) Jane Hazell
Production manager Carol Currie

Publisher Sue Wannan
Group publisher Jill Baker
Chief executive officer John Alexander

Produced by ACP Books, Sydney.

Colour separations by
ACP Colour Graphics Pty Ltd, Sydney.
Printing by Dai Nippon Printing, Hong Kong.

Published by ACP Publishing Pty Limited,
54 Park St, Sydney; GPO Box 4088, Sydney,
NSW 1028. Ph: (02) 9282 8618
Fax: (02) 9267 9438.

To order books, phone 136 116.
acpbooks@acp.com.au
www.acpbooks.com.au

Australia Distributed by Network Services,
GPO Box 4088, Sydney, NSW 1028.
Ph: (02) 9282 8777 Fax: (02) 9264 3278.

United Kingdom Distributed by Australian
Consolidated Press (UK), Moulton Park Business
Centre, Red House Road, Moulton Park,
Northampton, NN3 6AQ. Ph: (01604) 497 531
Fax: (01604) 497 533 acpukltd@aol.com

Canada Distributed by Whitecap Books Ltd,
351 Lynn Ave, North Vancouver, BC, V7J 2C4,
Ph: (604) 980 9852.

New Zealand Distributed by Netlink Distribution
Company, Level 4, 23 Hargreaves St,
College Hill, Auckland 1, Ph: (9) 302 7616.

South Africa Distributed by PSD Promotions
(Pty) Ltd, PO Box 1175, Isando 1600, SA.
Ph: (011) 392 6065.

Low-fat Gourmet.

Includes index.
ISBN 1 86396 272 7

1. Low-fat diet – recipes.
I. Title: Low-fat Gourmet. II. Title: Australian
Women's Weekly. (Series: Australian Women's
Weekly Healthy Eating mini series).

641.5635

© ACP Publishing Pty Limited 2002
ABN 18 053 273 546

Cover: Chilli-glazed spatchcock with
nori rice triangles, page 34
Stylist: Cherise Koch
Photographer: Joe Filshie
Back cover: Rich chocolate
meringue cake, page 45